TABLE OF CONTENTS

S0-ABA-820

Help the bus get to the zoo.
Draw a line to show the way.

COURTHOUSE

HOSPITAL

PARK

ZOO

Draw lines between the shapes that **match**.

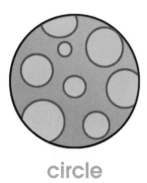

circle

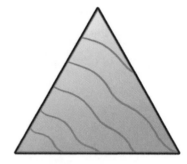

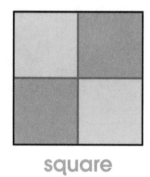

square

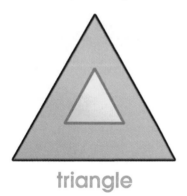

triangle

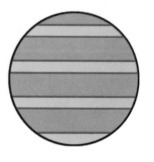

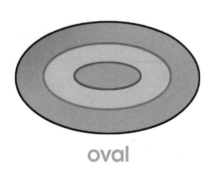

oval

Draw lines between the shapes that **match**.

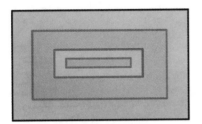

rectangle

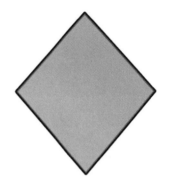

heart

diamond

star

Color the  green.

Color the s yellow.

Color the  blue.

Color the  purple.

Color the  orange.

Color the brown.

Color the  red.

Color the  black.

Leave the  white.

Draw a line from each word to the animal it describes.

small

LONG

tall

BIG

BIG & SMALL

Circle the animals you know to be big with a .
Circle the animals you know to be small with a .

Circle 6 hidden s.
Then color the picture.

10

WHICH ARE THE SAME?

These   are the **same**.

Circle the pictures that are the **same**.

Circle the letters that are the **same** as the first two.

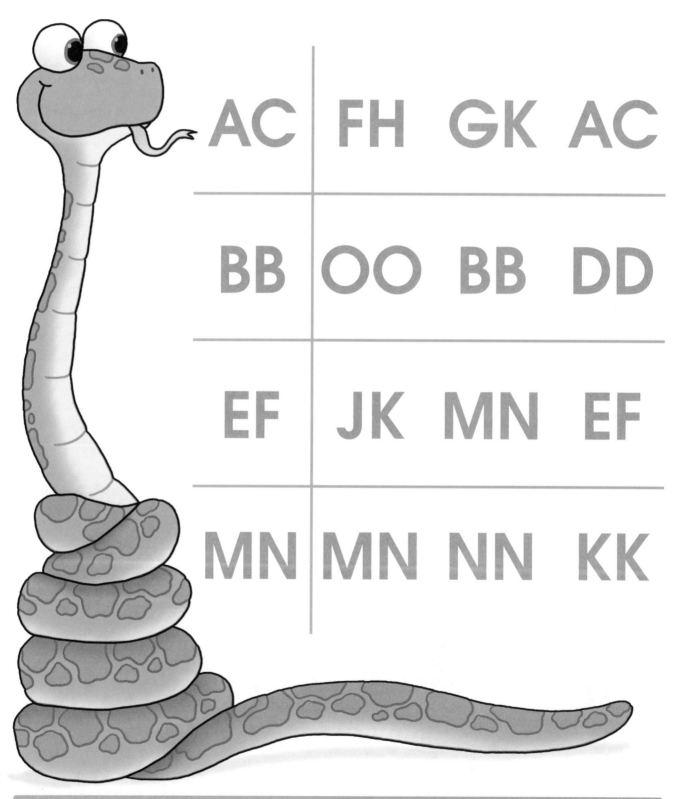

AC	FH	GK	AC
BB	OO	BB	DD
EF	JK	MN	EF
MN	MN	NN	KK

PERFECT PAIRS

A and a **make a pair**.

A and a **do not make a pair**.

Circle the pictures that **make a pair**.

 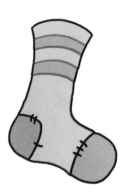  

 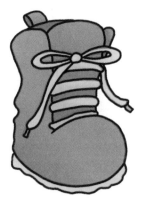  

A BIT DIFFERENT

This  and this are the **same**.

This  and this are **different**.

Circle the balloon that is **different**.

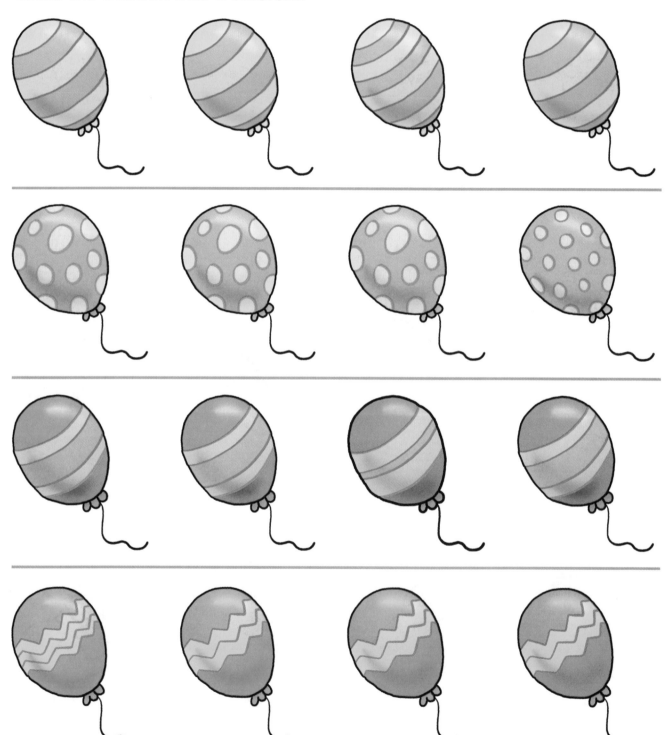

A BIT DIFFERENT

Circle the picture that is **different**.

GOES TOGETHER

 and 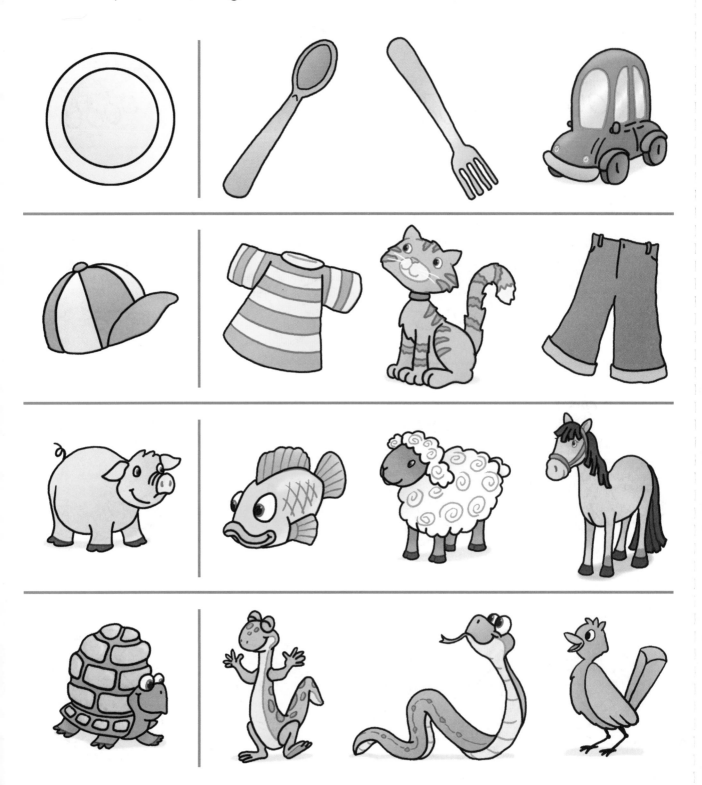 **go together.**

Circle the pictures that **go with** the first one.

Circle the pictures that **go with** the big one.

ODD ONE OUT

 and **do not belong** together.

Cross out the picture that **does not belong** with the first one.

 |

 |

 |

 |

Cross out the picture that **does not belong** with the big one.

Circle the picture that completes each sentence.

is to ___ as ___ is to _____ .

 is to  as  is to _____ .

Circle the picture that completes each sentence.

is to _____ as _____ is to _____ .

is to _____ as _____ is to _____ .

Draw a line from each picture to the weather that would make you use it.

BOOK BOUND

Draw a line from each picture to the book where you would find it.

Color the animals.
Circle the animals that have fur with a .
Circle the animals that have feathers with a .
Circle the animals that do not have feathers or fur with a .

Animals move in different ways.
Circle the animals that run with a 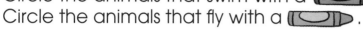.
Circle the animals that swim with a .
Circle the animals that fly with a .

Circle the picture that has something **missing**.
Draw the missing part.

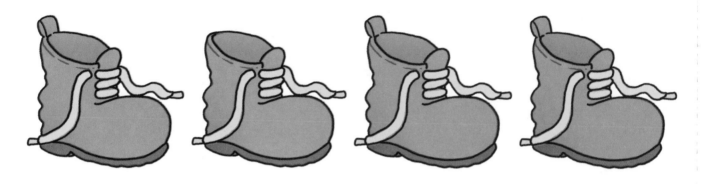

WHAT IS MISSING?

Circle the picture that has something **missing**.
Draw the missing part.

Circle the picture that has something **missing**.
Draw the missing part.

WHAT COMES NEXT?

Color the picture to continue the **pattern**.

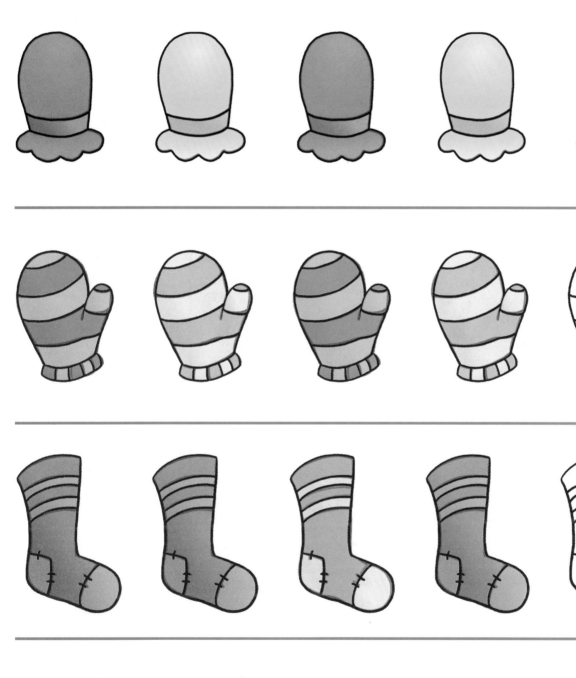

Circle the correct picture to continue the **pattern**.

WHAT COMES NEXT?

Circle the correct picture to continue the **pattern**.

Circle 5 silly things in the picture.

REAL & MAKE-BELIEVE

Circle the animals that look **real**.
Cross out the **make-believe** animals.

WHAT'S WRONG?

Circle 5 things that **do not belong** in the picture.

WHAT'S DIFFERENT?

Look at Picture A.
Circle 5 things that are **different** in Picture B.

PICTURE A

PICTURE B

Visual Discrimination

ALL THAT'S LEFT

This  is going **left**.

Circle the people who are going **left**.

ON THE RIGHT TRACK

This 🐰 is going **right**.

Circle the cars that are going **right**.

The bird is **in** the  .

Circle the things that are **in** something.

The bird is **out** of the  .

Circle the things that are **out** of something.

The  is **on** the table.

The is **by** the table.

The is **under** the table.

Draw an on the .

Draw a by the .

Draw a under the .

Circle how many you see.

How many s are **in** the ?   4   5   6

How many ✿s are **on** the ?   2   3   4

How many 🐶s are **under** the ?   1   2   3

STORY ORDER

Write **1** to show what happened **first**.
Write **2** to show what happened **next**.
Write **3** to show what happened **last**.

STORY ORDER

Write **1** to show what happened **first**.
Write **2** to show what happened **next**.
Write **3** to show what happened **last**.

Look at the big picture.
Why did this happen?
Circle the picture that shows **why**.

Look at the big picture.
Why did this happen?
Circle the picture that shows **why**.

CAUSE & EFFECT RELATIONSHIPS

Look at the big picture.
What do you think will happen?
Circle the picture that shows what will happen **next**.

48

Practice tracing the letters.

UNDER THE SEA

Connect the dots from **A** to **Z**.
Then color the picture.

A	B	C	D	E	F	G	H	I
J	K	L	M	N	O	P	Q	R
S	T	U	V	W	X	Y	Z	

Connect the dots from **A** to **Z**.
Then color the picture.

A	B	C	D	E	F	G	H	I
J	K	L	M	N	O	P	Q	R
S	T	U	V	W	X	Y	Z	

Circle the picture whose name begins with the **same sound** as the first one.

Bb
ball

Ff
feather

Kk
key

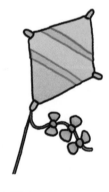

Nn
nuts

BEGINNING SOUNDS

Circle the picture whose name begins with the **same sound** as the first one.

Dd
doll

Zz
zipper

Ll
leaf

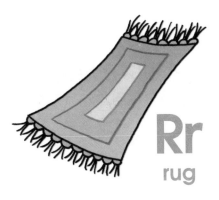

Rr
rug

BEGINNING SOUNDS

Circle the picture whose name begins with the **same sound** as the first one.

 **Vv** vase

 **Jj** jack-o'-lantern
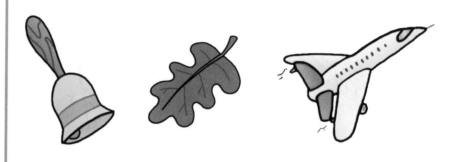

 **Pp** pizza

 **Ss** socks

BEGINNING SOUNDS

Circle the picture whose name begins with the **same sound** as the first one.

BEGINNING SOUNDS

Circle the picture whose name begins with the **same sound** as the first one.

 **Cc** cow |

 **Gg** goose |

 **Hh** hat |

 **Qq** quarter |

  **Xx** x-ray

Star **rhymes** with car.

Circle the picture that **rhymes** with the first one.

bear

pig

pear

goat

boat

moon

frog

dog

rabbit

fox

box

fish

MORE RHYME TIME

Circle the picture that **rhymes** with the first one.

cat

monkey

bat

bee

tree

dolphin

snake

cake

alligator

stork

panda

fork

Count the fruit. Trace the numbers.

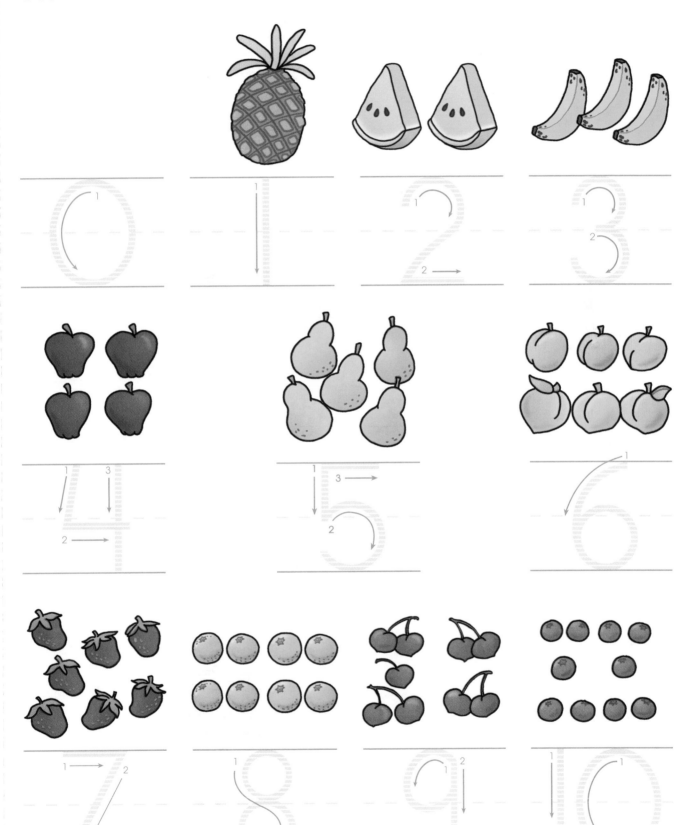

ZERO

Trace and write the number.

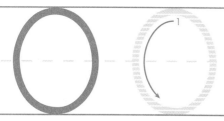

Write how many there are.

_____

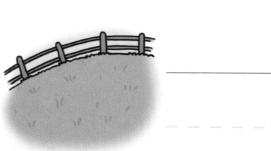

_____

_____

_____

_____

_____

Trace and write the numbers.

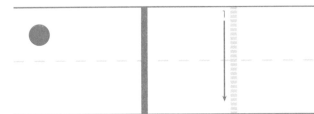

Write how many there are.

Trace and write the numbers.

3 3 3

4 4 4

Write how many there are.

 _____

 _____

 _____

 _____

 _____

 _____

IN THE PARK

Circle **1** hidden .

Circle **2** hidden ~~~~s.

Circle **3** hidden s.

Circle **4** hidden s.

Trace and write the numbers.

Write how many there are.

How many are there?
Take a guess. Then count.

My Guess			
My Count			

FAMILY COUNTS

Circle how many babies you see in the pictures.

Trace and write the numbers.

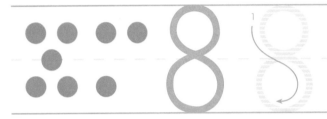

Write how many there are.

COUNTING CRITTERS

Circle how many you see.

How many 🐧s are there?   **6 7 8**

How many 🐨s are there?   **5 6 7**

How many 🦩s are there?   **4 5 6**

How many s are there? **2 3 4**

How many s are there? **5 6 7**

How many s are there? **0 1 2**

Trace and write the numbers.

Write how many there are.

Connect the dots from **1** to **10**.
Then color the picture.

Connect the dots from 1 to 10.
Then color the picture.

2 is **before** 3.

(2) 3 4

0 1 2 3 4 5 6 7 8 9 10

Write the number that comes **before**.

_____

4 5

_____

5 6

_____

6 7

_____

1 2

_____

7 8

_____

9 10

_____

8 9

_____

3 4

2 is **between** 1 and 3.

1 ② 3

0 1 2 3 4 5 6 7 8 9 10

Write the number that comes **between**.

3 ____ 5		2 ____ 4	
6 ____ 8		5 ____ 7	
4 ____ 6		8 ____ 10	
7 ____ 9		1 ____ 3	

6 comes **after** 5.

4   5   ⑥

0 1 2 3 4 5 6 7 8 9 10

Write the number that comes **after**.

5 6 _____	2 3 _____
_____ 7 8 _____	_____ 6 7 _____
_____ 8 9 _____	_____ 4 5 _____
_____ 3 4 _____	_____ 0 1 _____

SAME AMOUNT

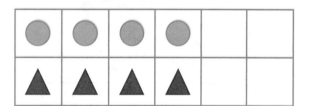

How many s are there? **(4)** 5 6

How many ▲s are there? **(4)** 5 6

Draw s to show the **same** number as s.

How many s are there? **1   2   3**

How many s are there? **1   2   3**

Draw s to show the **same** number as s.

How many s are there? **4   5   6**

How many s are there? **4   5   6**

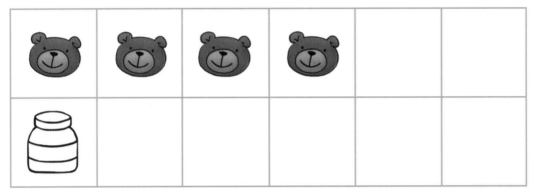

How many s are there? **③ 4 5**

How many s are there? **3 ④ 5**

Draw s to show **one more** than s.

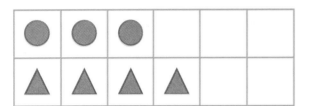

How many s are there? **4 5 6**

How many s are there? **4 5 6**

Draw to show **one more** than s.

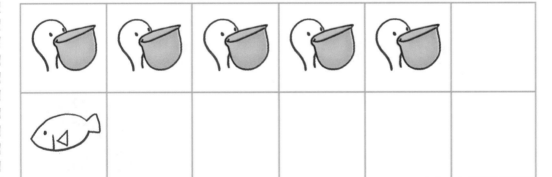

How many s are there? **4 5 6**

How many are there? **4 5 6**

How many ⬤s are there?   2   ③   4

How many ▲s are there?   ②   3   4

Draw 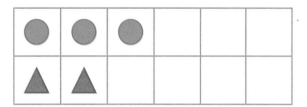s to show **one fewer** 🥕 than 🐰s.

How many 🐰s are there?   **4   5   6**

How many 🥕s are there?   **4   5   6**

Draw 🥚s to show **one fewer** 🥚 than 🐦s.

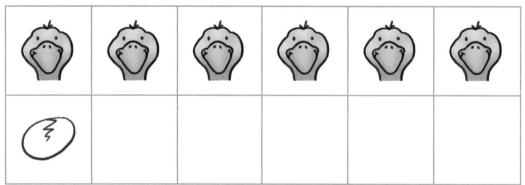

How many 🐦s are there?   **4   5   6**

How many 🥚s are there?   **4   5   6**

MORE OR FEWER?

How many s are there? **4 5 6**

How many s are there? **4 5 6**

Circle which has **more**.

How many s are there? **4 5 6**

How many s are there? **4 5 6**

Circle which has **fewer**.

Greater means **more than**.
4 is **greater than** 3.

Write how many there are.
Circle the set that has a **greater** number.

 _____   _____

_____ _____

 _____  _____

_____ _____

 _____  _____

_____ _____

Draw a set of s to show 1 **more than** 3. _____

_____

How many s are there? _____

MORE FRUIT

Circle the set that has a **greater** number.

2 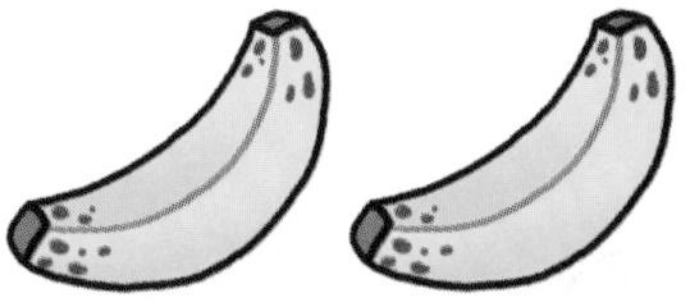

3 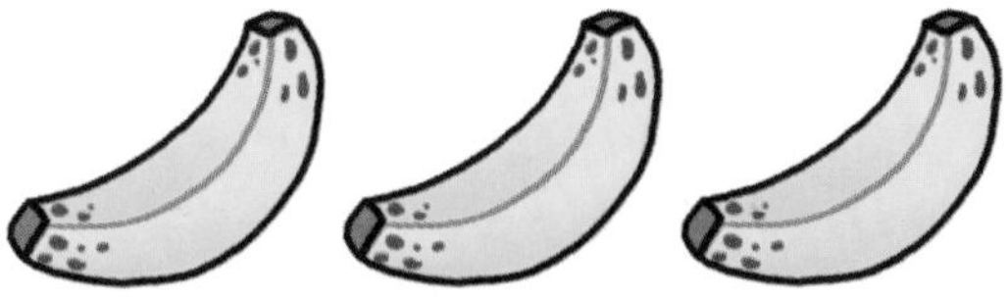

---

9 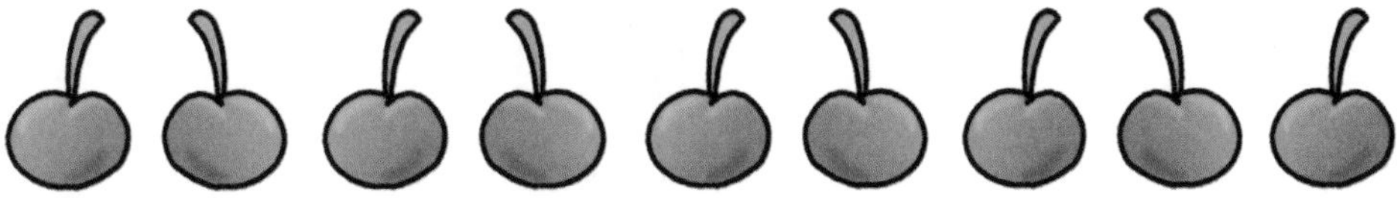

6 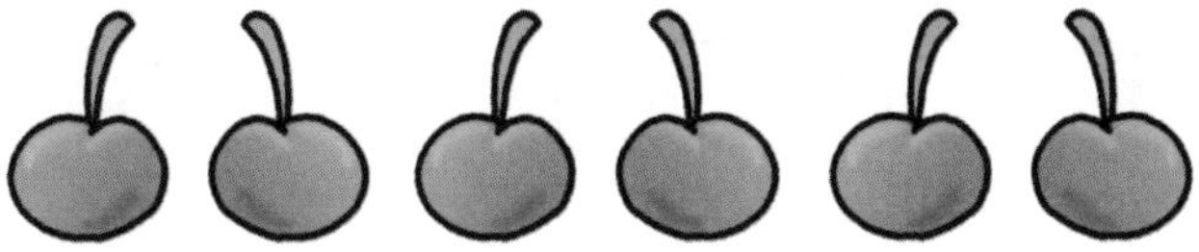

---

8 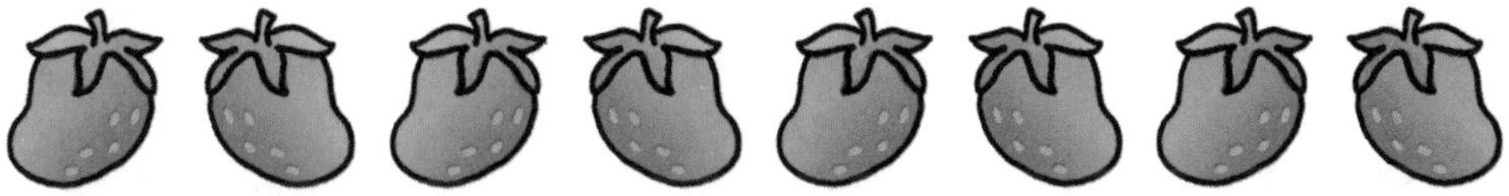

7 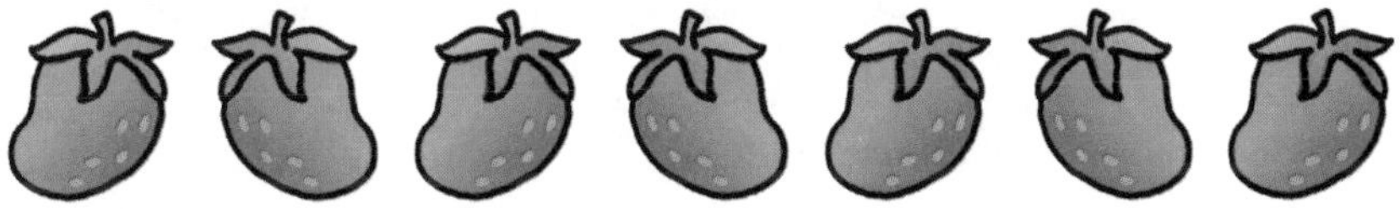

---

6 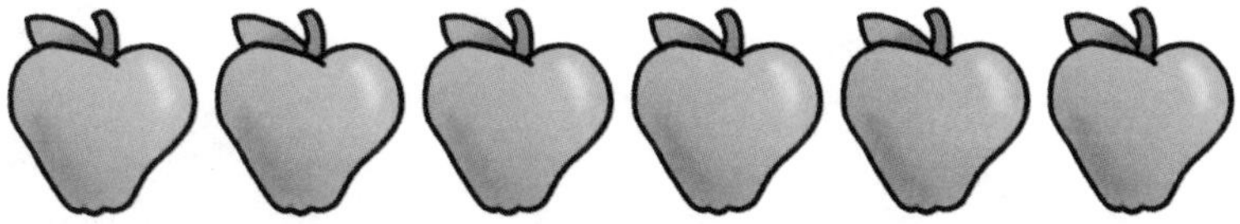

8 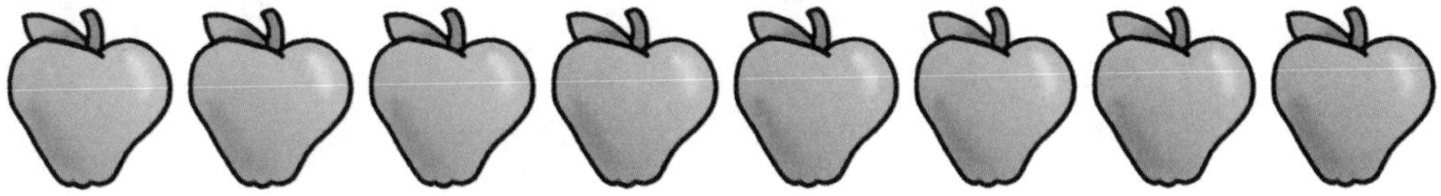

Circle the set that has **one more than** the first set.

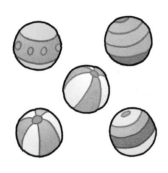  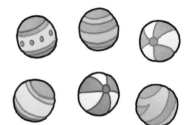

  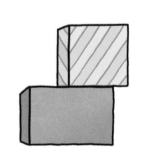

Less means **fewer** or **not as many**.
2 is **less than** 3.

Write how many there are.
Circle the set that has **fewer**.

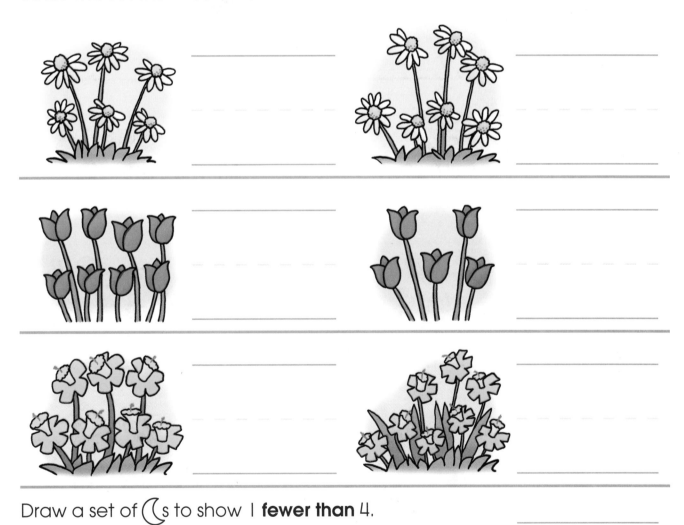

Draw a set of (s to show 1 **fewer than** 4.

How many (s are there? _____

Circle the set that has **fewer**.

3

2

4

6

5

7

8

9

4

3

9

7

FEWER FOOD GROUPS

Circle the set that has **one less than** the first set.

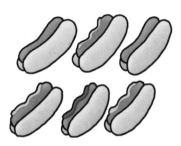 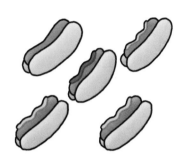 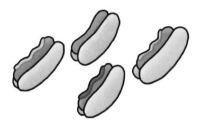

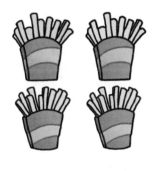  

Write how many there are **altogether**.

1 + 2 = __3__

3 + 1 = _____   2 + 3 = _____

3 + 3 = _____   4 + 3 = _____

4 + 2 = _____   5 + 2 = _____

Write how many are **left**.

$$3 - 1 = \underline{\quad 2 \quad}$$

$$3 - 2 = \underline{\qquad}$$

$$4 - 2 = \underline{\qquad}$$

$$5 - 3 = \underline{\qquad}$$

$$6 - 4 = \underline{\qquad}$$

$$5 - 2 = \underline{\qquad}$$

$$6 - 2 = \underline{\qquad}$$

Subtraction

TICK-TOCK

Write the numbers on the clock.
Color the long hand **blue**.
Color the short hand **red**.

12

Minute Hand

Hour Hand

When the hour hand points to the 3 and the minute hand points to the 12, it is 3 o'clock.

Hour → **3**
_____

3
_____ o'clock

The short hand tells the hours.
Where does the hour hand point?

Hour →
_____

_____ o'clock

Hour →
_____

_____ o'clock

Hour →
_____

_____ o'clock

Hour →
_____

_____ o'clock

Hour →
_____

_____ o'clock

Hour →
_____

_____ o'clock

COUNTING COINS

I Penny
I Cent
I¢

Count the pennies. Write how many there are.

 _____ ¢

  _____ ¢

  _____ ¢

 _____ ¢

$$3¢ + 1¢$$
_____ ¢

$$2¢ + 2¢$$
_____ ¢

MAKING AMOUNTS

Read the number on the price tag.
Circle that many pennies.
The first one is done for you.

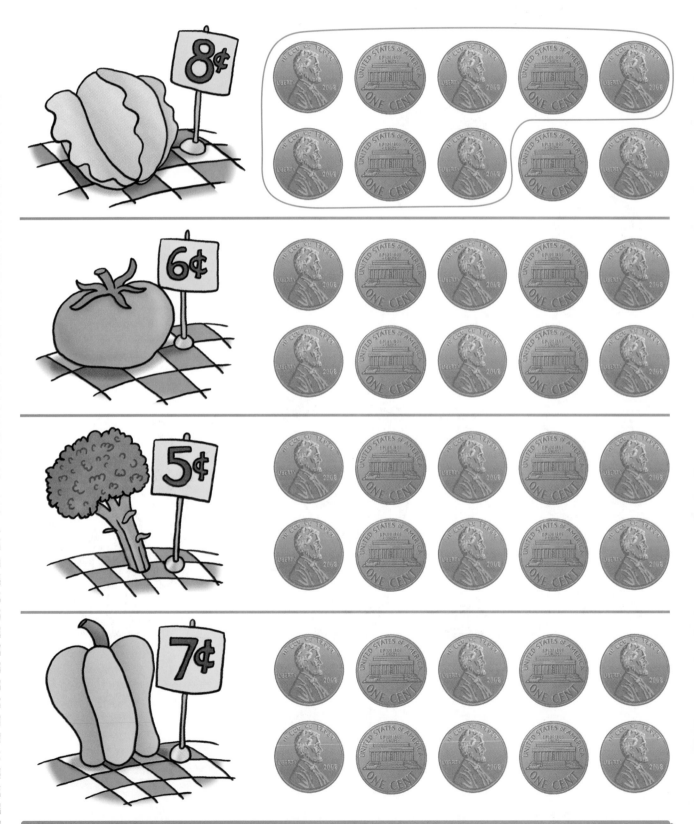

Measure each family member. Use a .

How many s tall is each one?

ONE-HALF

Look at the shape. It has 2 equal parts.
Each part is **one-half** or $\frac{1}{2}$.

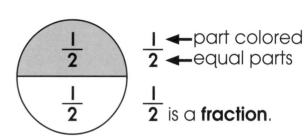

$\frac{1}{2}$ ←part colored
$\frac{1}{2}$ ←equal parts

$\frac{1}{2}$ is a **fraction**.

Color **one-half** $\left(\frac{1}{2}\right)$ of each shape.
The first one is done for you.

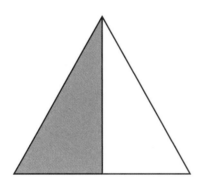

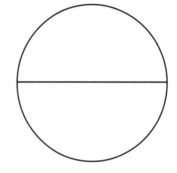

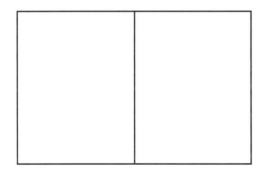

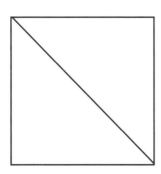

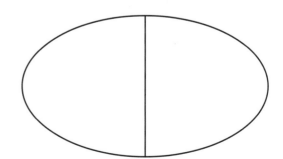

Look at the shape. It has 3 equal parts.
Each part is **one-third** or $\frac{1}{3}$.

$\frac{1}{3}$ ←part colored
←equal parts

| $\frac{1}{3}$ | $\frac{1}{3}$ | $\frac{1}{3}$ |

$\frac{1}{3}$ is a **fraction**.

Color **one-third** $\left(\frac{1}{3}\right)$ of each shape.
The first one is done for you.

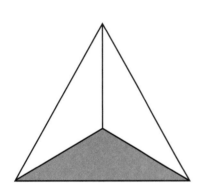

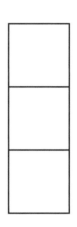

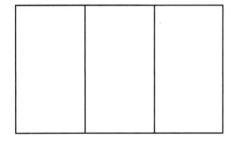

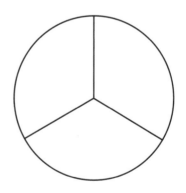

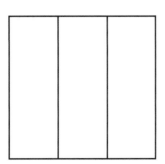

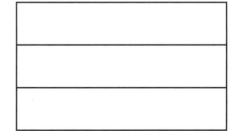

Look at the shape. It has 4 equal parts.
Each part is **one-fourth** or $\frac{1}{4}$.

$\frac{1}{4}$ ← part colored
$\frac{1}{4}$ ← equal parts

$\frac{1}{4}$ is a **fraction**.

Color **one-fourth** $\left(\frac{1}{4}\right)$ of each shape.
The first one is done for you.

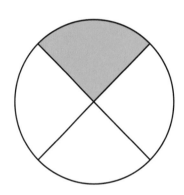

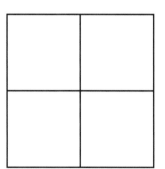

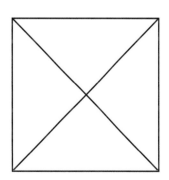

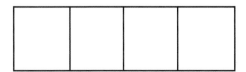

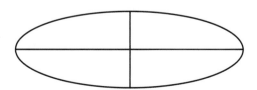

AWARD

Great Job!

_____
Name

finished Kindergarten Basics
from
School Zone Publishing Company.